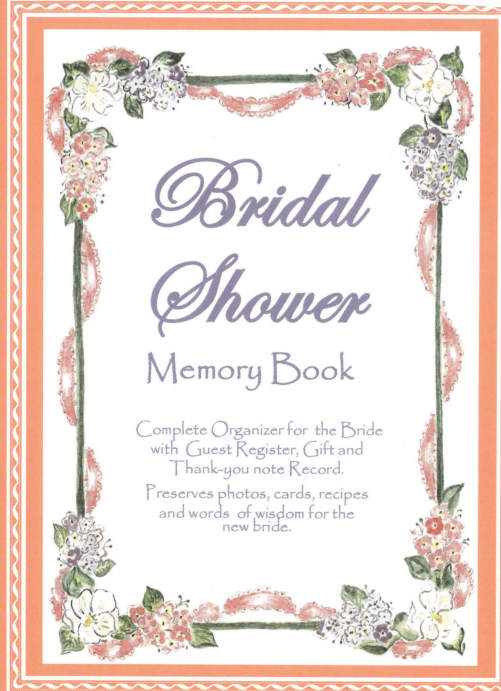

Bridal Shower
Memory Book

Complete Organizer for the Bride with Guest Register, Gift and Thank-you note Record.

Preserves photos, cards, recipes and words of wisdom for the new bride.

©Traditions Press, Inc. 2017
Bridal Shower Memory Book
www.traditionspress.com
designed and illustrated by n s taylor
traditionspress@gmail.com
Lexington, SC USA

ISBN # 13: 978-1537412887

ISBN 10: 1537412884

Bridal Shower

Memories

of

_____

Photo

Shower Invitation

By having an individual designated to greet guests and direct them to sign the Guest Registry, it will help insure that the bride has a current and complete address to expedite writing thank you notes.

(A thoughtful gift for the bride would be a couple of boxes of thank you notes and several sheets of the beautiful postage stamps that are available.)

Guests

Name	Address	Phone	email

Guests

Name	Address	Phone	email

Guests

Name	Address	Phone	email

Guests

Name	Address	Phone	email

Gift Registry

As gifts are being opened another attendant should be recording the gift and the person's name who brought the gift. This is an immensely helpful service for the bride. A secure satchel or box for checks, gift cards and other monetary gifts is good to have available to help keep up with financial gifts.

After the shower when it is time to start the task of writing thank you notes the bride will appreciate having complete information available.

Gift Register

Gift	Given by	Acknowledgement Sent

Gift Register

Gift	Given by	Acknowledgement Sent

Gift Register

Gift	Given by	Acknowledgement Sent

Gift Register

Gift	Given by	Acknowledgement Sent

Gift Register

Gift	Given by	Acknowledgement Sent

Gift Register

Gift	Given by	Acknowledgement Sent

Gift Register

Gift	Given by	Acknowledgement Sent

Gift Register

Gift	Given by	Acknowledgement Sent

Gift Register

Gift	Given by	Acknowledgement Sent

Gift Register

Gift	Given by	Acknowledgement Sent

Words of Wisdom for the Bride

This section of the book may be used by guests to write helpful sayings, quotations, scripture and other helpful words for the bride. Expressions of hope, encouragement and sharing will be appreciated as they offer personal messages preserved for the bride to discover in years to come.

(The hostess might want to include in the invitation a request that attendees bring a special quote to go in this book for the bride.)

Words of Wisdom for the Bride

_____
_____
_____
Contributed by

_____
_____
_____
Contributed by

_____
_____
_____
Contributed by

_____
_____
_____
Contributed by

Words of Wisdom for the Bride

_____
_____
_____

Contributed by

_____
_____
_____

Contributed by

_____
_____
_____

Contributed by

_____
_____
_____

Contributed by

Words of Wisdom for the Bride

_____
_____
_____
Contributed by

_____
_____
_____
Contributed by

_____
_____
_____
Contributed by

_____
_____
_____
Contributed by

Words of Wisdom for the Bride

Contributed by

Contributed by

Contributed by

Contributed by

Words of Wisdom for the Bride

_____
_____
_____
Contributed by

_____
_____
_____
Contributed by

_____
_____
_____
Contributed by

_____
_____
_____
Contributed by

Words of Wisdom for the Bride

_____
_____
_____
Contributed by

_____
_____
_____
Contributed by

_____
_____
_____
Contributed by

_____
_____
_____
Contributed by

Recipes

always serve each other with love

A few special recipes would be a thoughtful gift to include in this album. Especially a family recipe for the bride or groom from their in-laws to be. Also, family recipes that are handed down through generations would have special meaning.

(The hostess might also want to suggest in the shower invitation that guests are encouraged to bring a recipe.)

...always serve each other with love...

Recipe _____

Contributed by _____

Ingredients: _____

_____

_____

_____

Directions: _____

_____

_____

_____

_____

_____

_____

_____

_____

_____

Recipe _____

Contributed by _____

Ingredients: _____

_____

_____

_____

Directions: _____

_____

_____

_____

_____

_____

_____

_____

_____

_____

...always serve each other with love...

Recipe _____

Contributed by _____

Ingredients: _____

_____

_____

_____

_____

Directions: _____

_____

_____

_____

_____

_____

_____

_____

_____

Recipe _____

Contributed by _____

Ingredients: _____

_____

_____

_____

_____

Directions: _____

_____

_____

_____

_____

_____

_____

_____

_____

...always serve each other with love...

Recipe _____

Contributed by _____

Ingredients: _____
_____
_____
_____
_____

Directions: _____
_____
_____
_____
_____
_____
_____
_____
_____

Recipe _____

Contributed by _____

Ingredients: _____
_____
_____
_____
_____

Directions: _____
_____
_____
_____
_____
_____
_____
_____
_____

...always serve each other with love...

Recipe _____

Contributed by _____

Ingredients: _____

_____
_____
_____
_____

Directions: _____

_____
_____
_____
_____
_____
_____
_____
_____

Recipe _____

Contributed by _____

Ingredients: _____

_____
_____
_____
_____

Directions: _____

_____
_____
_____
_____
_____
_____
_____
_____

...always serve each other with love...

Recipe _____
Contributed by _____
Ingredients: _____
_____
_____
_____

Directions: _____
_____
_____
_____
_____
_____
_____
_____
_____

Recipe _____
Contributed by _____
Ingredients: _____
_____
_____
_____

Directions: _____
_____
_____
_____
_____
_____
_____
_____
_____

...always serve each other with love...

Recipe _____

Contributed by _____

Ingredients: _____

_____

_____

_____

_____

Directions: _____

_____

_____

_____

_____

_____

_____

_____

_____

_____

Recipe _____

Contributed by _____

Ingredients: _____

_____

_____

_____

_____

Directions: _____

_____

_____

_____

_____

_____

_____

_____

_____

_____

...always serve each other with love...

Recipe _____

Contributed by _____

Ingredients: _____

_____

_____

_____

Directions: _____

_____

_____

_____

_____

_____

_____

_____

_____

Recipe _____

Contributed by _____

Ingredients: _____

_____

_____

_____

Directions: _____

_____

_____

_____

_____

_____

_____

_____

_____

...always serve each other with love...

Recipe _____

Contributed by _____

Ingredients: _____

_____

_____

_____

_____

Directions: _____

_____

_____

_____

_____

_____

_____

_____

_____

_____

Recipe _____

Contributed by _____

Ingredients: _____

_____

_____

_____

_____

Directions: _____

_____

_____

_____

_____

_____

_____

_____

_____

...always serve each other with love...

Recipe _____

Contributed by _____

Ingredients: _____

_____

_____

_____

Directions: _____

_____

_____

_____

_____

_____

_____

_____

_____

Recipe _____

Contributed by _____

Ingredients: _____

_____

_____

_____

Directions: _____

_____

_____

_____

_____

_____

_____

_____

_____

...always serve each other with love...

Recipe _____

Contributed by _____

Ingredients: _____
_____
_____
_____
_____

Directions: _____
_____
_____
_____
_____
_____
_____
_____
_____

Recipe _____

Contributed by _____

Ingredients: _____
_____
_____
_____
_____

Directions: _____
_____
_____
_____
_____
_____
_____
_____
_____

Displaying Gifts

At the Shower a table may be decorated with a suitable covering and trimmings. The gifts may be placed on the table after being opened and recorded in the gift registry. Small cards may be placed by the gifts with the name of the person giving the gift. A dinner place card is a good size for this job. Care in keeping cards with gifts should be taken when packing the gifts after the shower. There are many attractive, inexpensive large bags that are great for helping the bride to pack and transport her gifts.

Thank You Notes

As time and circumstances dictate, thank you notes should be written for each gift. This should be done in the form of a handwritten note within one year of receiving the gift. Simple note cards are sufficient; and it is good to name the specific gift. In the note. Appreciation may be expressed about the usefulness, matching colors and special thoughtfulness of the gift. Notes need not be long letters.

(Husbands can write thank you notes too!)

Books, Websites and other sources...

Books, Websites and other sources...

Mementos, Product Warranties, Notes

Mementos, Product Warranties, Notes

Mementos, Product Warranties, Notes

Mementos, Product Warranties, Notes

Important Family Dates

Birthdays, Anniversaries...

Important Family Dates

Birthdays, Anniversaries...

Made in the USA
Coppell, TX
07 August 2022